The World's Fastest Book

Jimmy Huston

Fast Edition

Copyright © 2025 Jimmy Huston

ISBN: 978-1-965153-72-7

Cosworth Publishing
21545 Yucatan Avenue
Woodland Hills CA 91364
www.cosworthpublishing.com

FOR INFORMATION REGARDING PERMISSION,
PLEASE SEND AN EMAIL TO
OFFICE@COSWORTHPUBLISHING.COM

Dedicated to Speedy Gonzales

Preface

Skip it.

Chapter One

Quick! Turn the page. ***Hurry!***

The End

WHOOSH

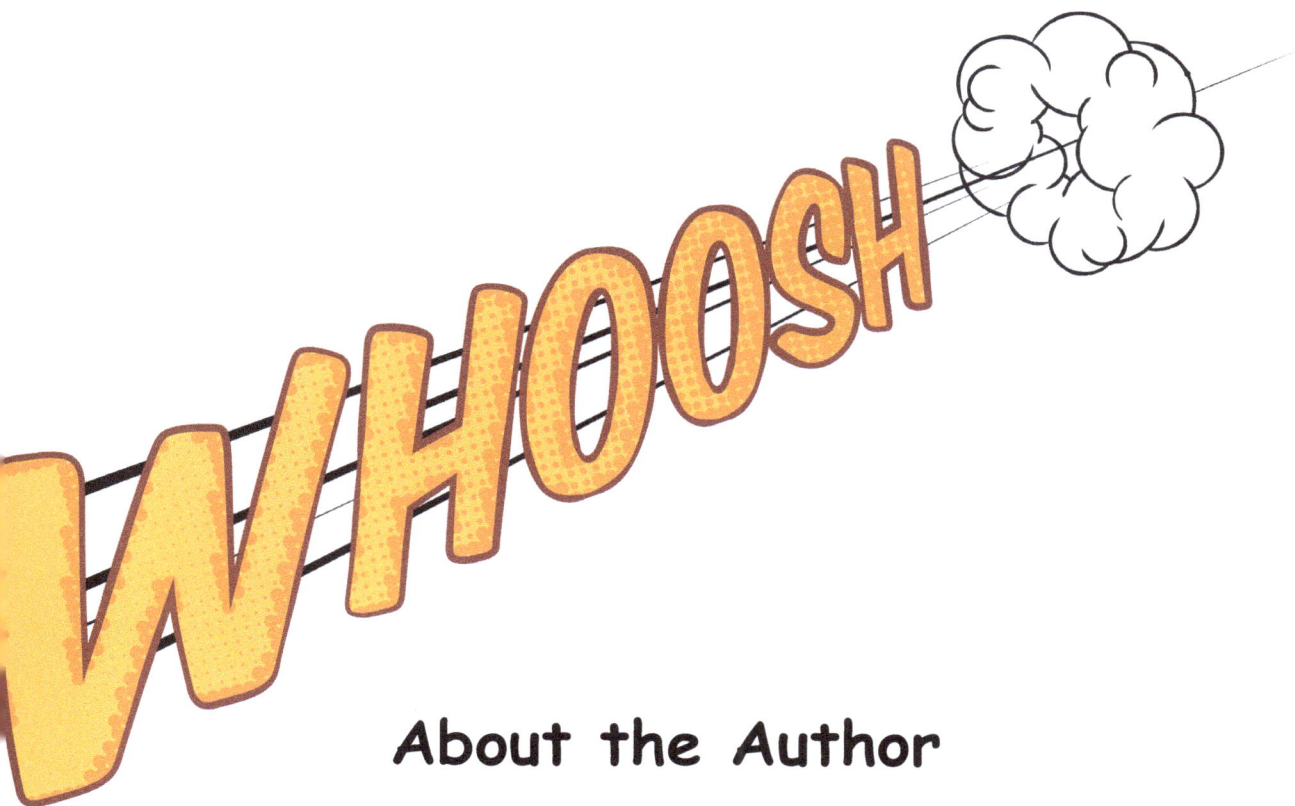

About the Author

Gone.

He's already on book two of the Fastest Book series.

And probably books three and four.

He's loco.

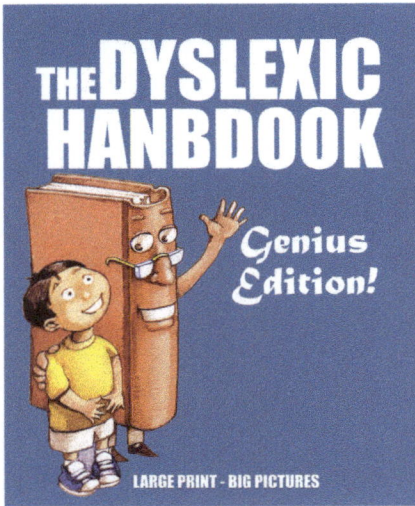

THE **DYSLEXIC HANBDOOK**
Genius Edition!
LARGE PRINT - BIG PICTURES

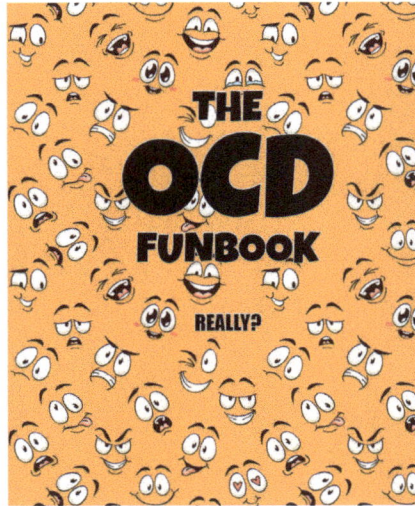

THE **OCD** FUNBOOK
REALLY?

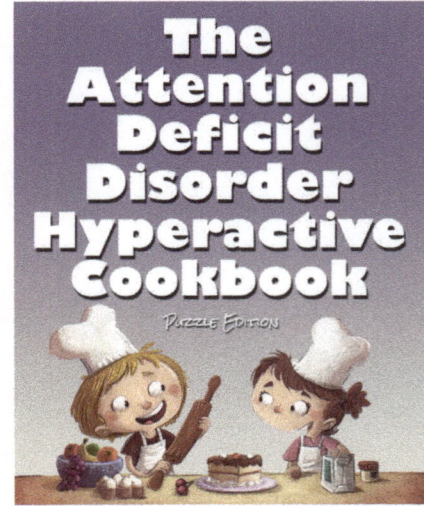

The **Attention Deficit Disorder Hyperactive Cookbook**
Puzzle Edition

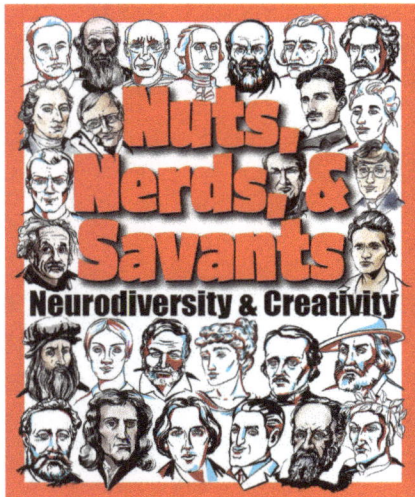

Nuts, Nerds, & Savants
Neurodiversity & Creativity

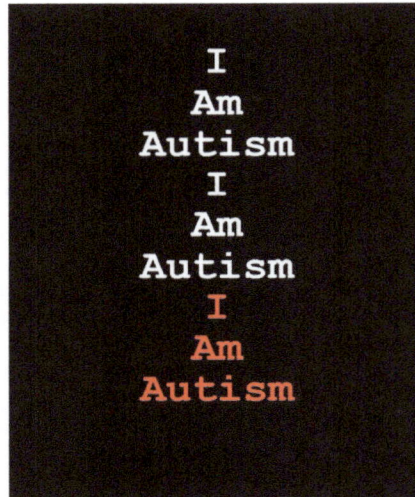

I Am Autism
I Am Autism
I Am Autism

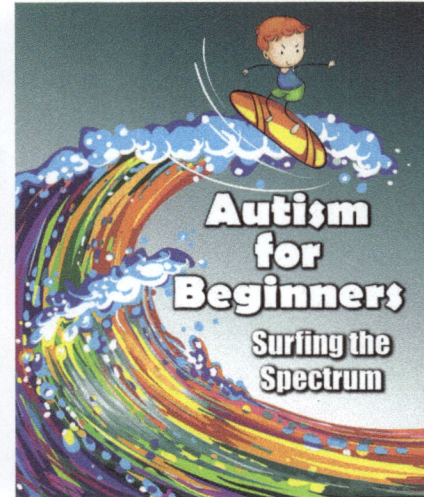

Autism for Beginners
Surfing the Spectrum

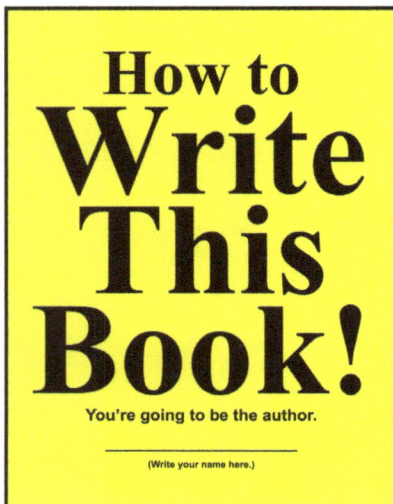

How to **Write This Book!**
You're going to be the author.
_____
(Write your name here.)

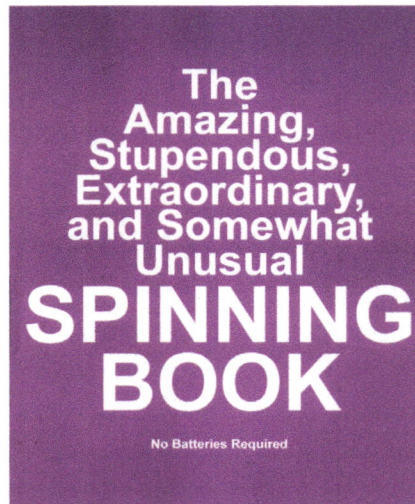

The Amazing, Stupendous, Extraordinary, and Somewhat Unusual **SPINNING BOOK**
No Batteries Required

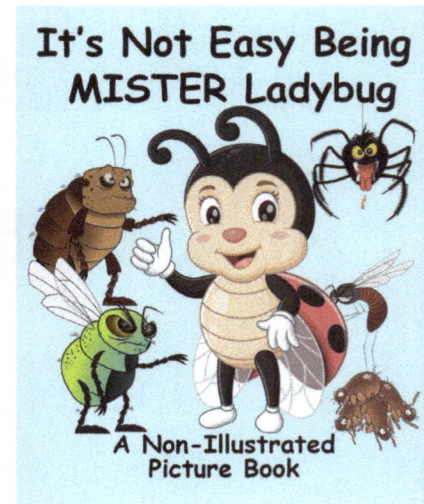

It's Not Easy Being MISTER Ladybug
A Non-Illustrated Picture Book

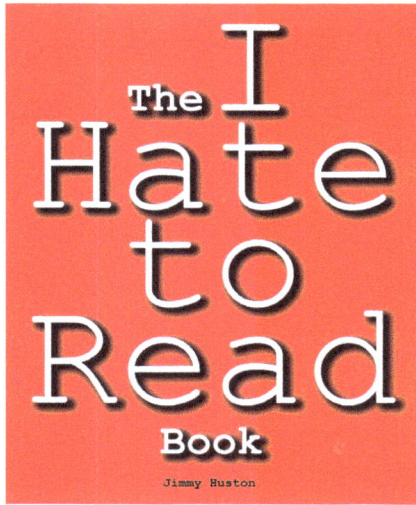

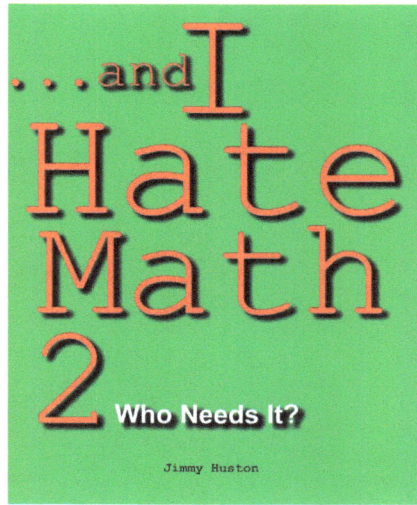

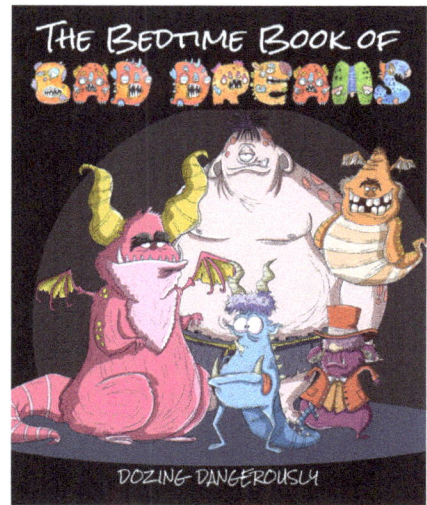

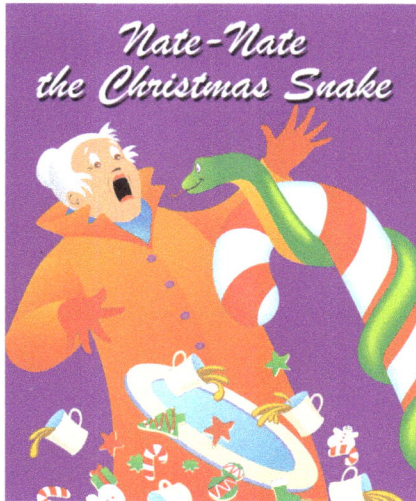

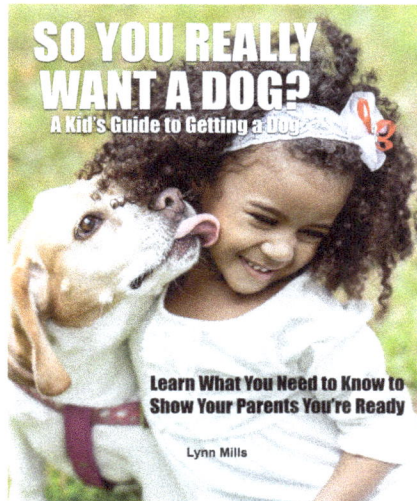

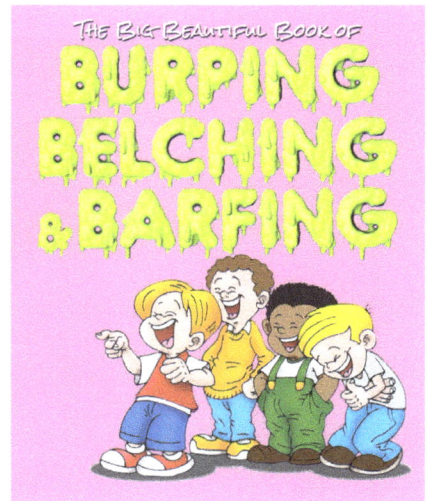

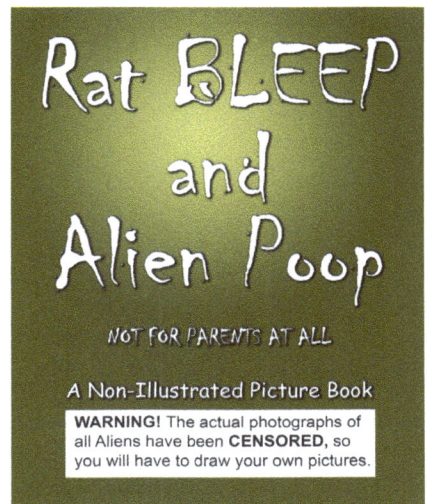

The **I** Hate to Read Book

Jimmy Huston

...and **I** Hate Math **2**

Who Needs It?

Jimmy Huston

THE BEDTIME BOOK OF **BAD DREAMS**

DOZING DANGEROUSLY

Nate-Nate the Christmas Snake

SO YOU REALLY WANT A DOG?
A Kid's Guide to Getting a Dog

Learn What You Need to Know to Show Your Parents You're Ready

Lynn Mills

THE BIG BEAUTIFUL BOOK OF **BURPING BELCHING & BARFING**

Why Can't Mommy Spend More Time with Me?

The Snake Test

☐ True? ☐ False? ☐ Maybe

Rat BLEEP and Alien Poop

NOT FOR PARENTS AT ALL

A Non-Illustrated Picture Book

WARNING! The actual photographs of all Aliens have been **CENSORED**, so you will have to draw your own pictures.

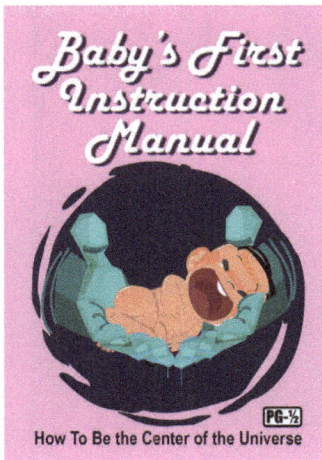

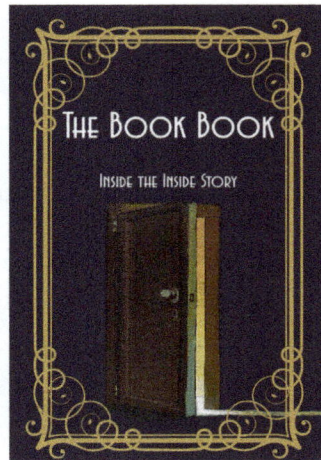

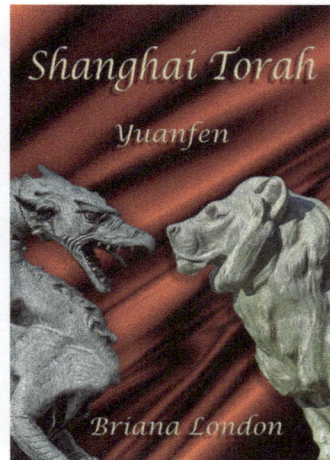

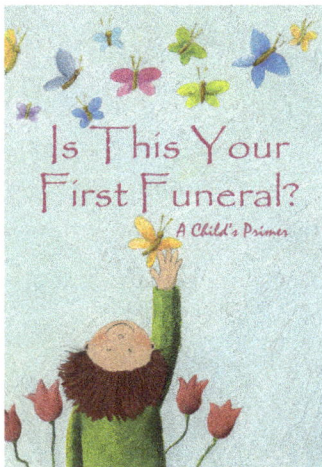

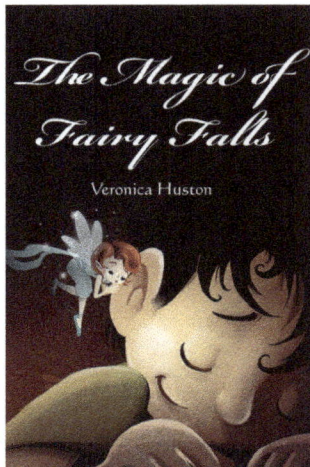

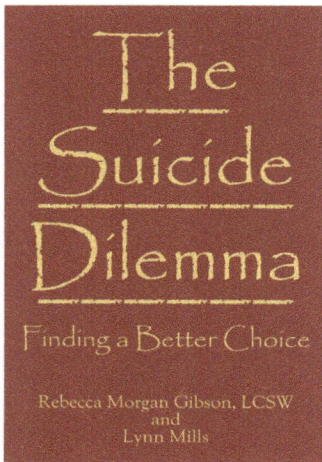

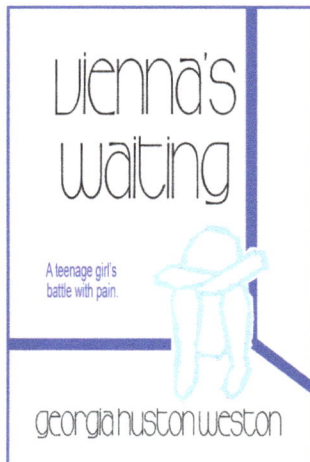

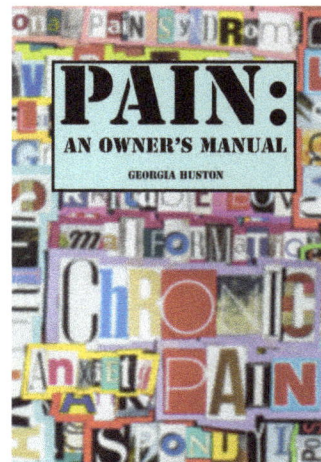

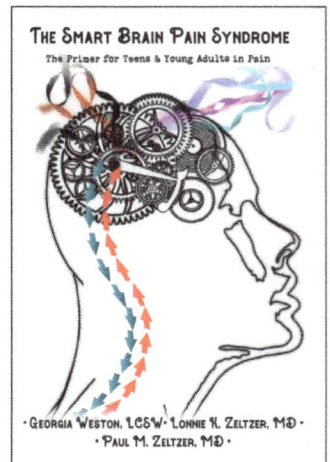

Baby's First Instruction Manual
PG-½
How To Be the Center of the Universe

The First Apology Is the Worst
Let's Get It Over With

THE BOOK BOOK
INSIDE THE INSIDE STORY

Shanghai Torah
Yuanfen
Briana London

Is This Your First Funeral?
A Child's Primer

The Magic of Fairy Falls
Veronica Huston

DON'T GO TO COLLEGE, GO TO EUROPE FOR LESS
Jimmy Huston

That Strange Little Angel!

The Suicide Dilemma
Finding a Better Choice
Rebecca Morgan Gibson, LCSW
and
Lynn Mills

vienna's waiting
A teenage girl's battle with pain.
georgia huston weston

PAIN: AN OWNER'S MANUAL
GEORGIA HUSTON
CHRONIC PAIN

THE SMART BRAIN PAIN SYNDROME
The Primer for Teens & Young Adults in Pain
· GEORGIA WESTON, LCSW· LONNIE K. ZELTZER, MD ·
· PAUL M. ZELTZER, MD ·

More Books from Cosworth Publishing
www.cosworthpublishing.com

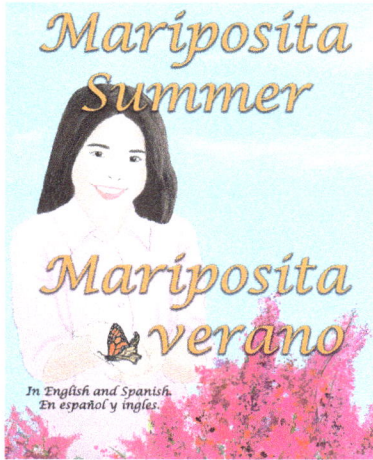

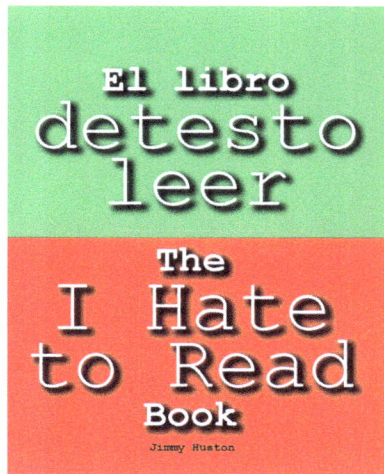

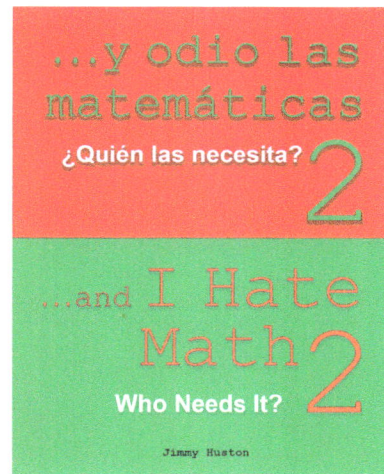

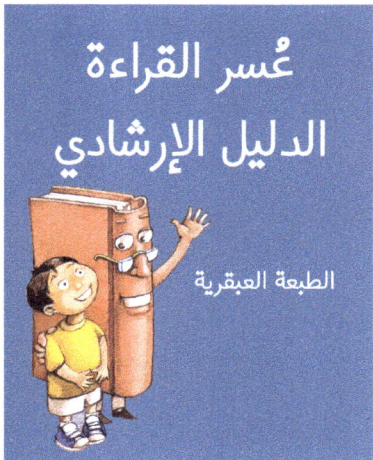

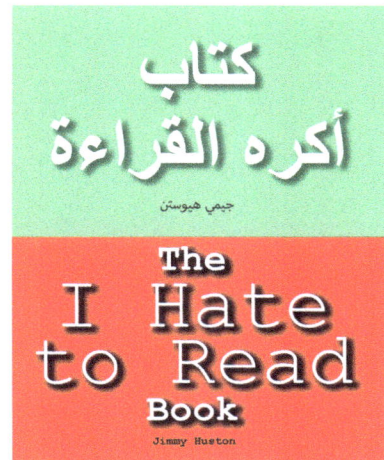

Mariposita Summer
Mariposita verano
In English and Spanish.
En español y inglés.

Wisdom of the Aged
PG-65
Dead Is the New Sick
An Insider's Guide to Senility,
Paranoia & Curmudgery
Jimmy Huston

CUSSING for KIDS!
Etiquette for the Profane

Engelmann the Footloose Christmas Spruce
Lynn Mills

El libro detesto leer
The I Hate to Read Book
Jimmy Huston

...y odio las matemáticas
¿Quién las necesita? **2**
...and I Hate Math 2
Who Needs It?
Jimmy Huston

عُسر القراءة
الدليل الإرشادي
الطبعة العبقرية

الكتاب الدوّار
المذهل، الرائع،
الاستثنائي قليلاً
لا توجد حاجة لاستخدام بطاريات
The Amazing, Stupendous,
Extraordinary, and Somewhat
Unusual
SPINNING BOOK
No Batteries Required
Jimmy Huston

كتاب
أكره القراءة
جيمي هيوستن
The I Hate to Read Book
Jimmy Huston

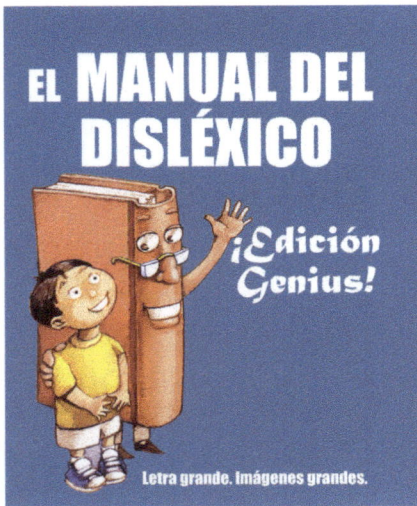
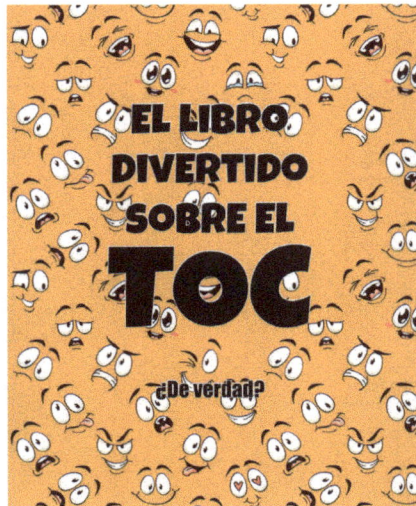

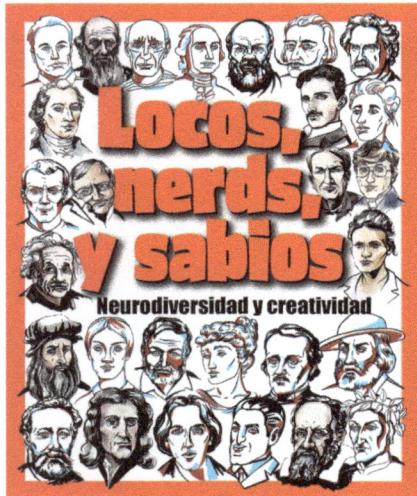
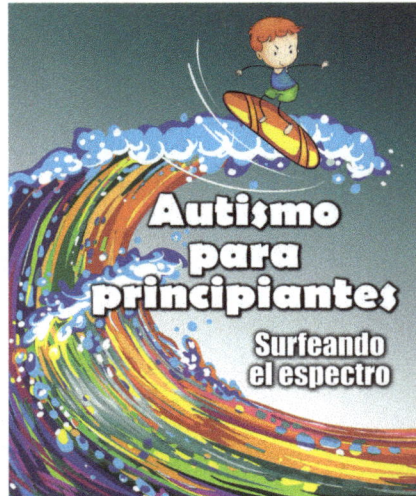
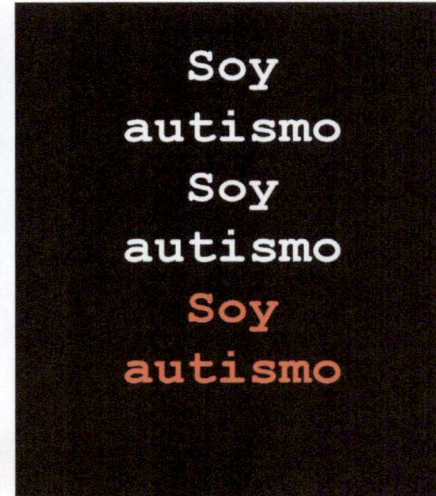
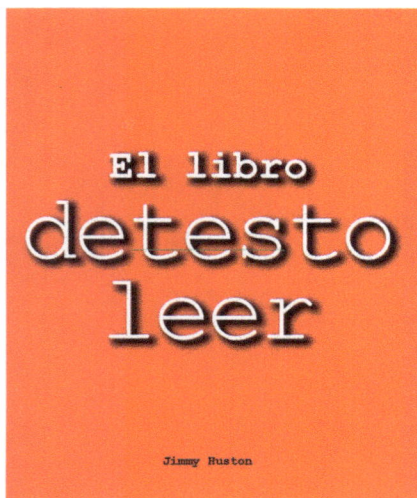
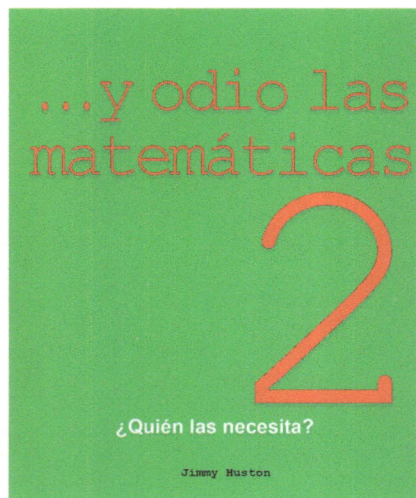

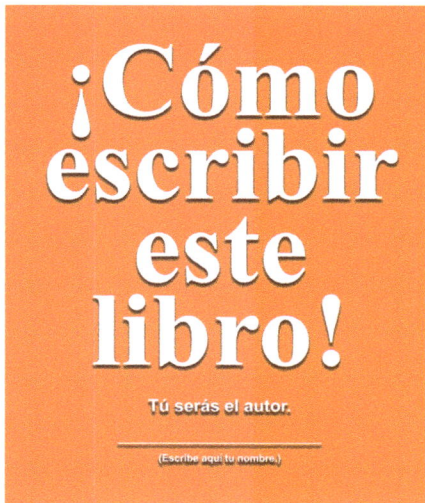

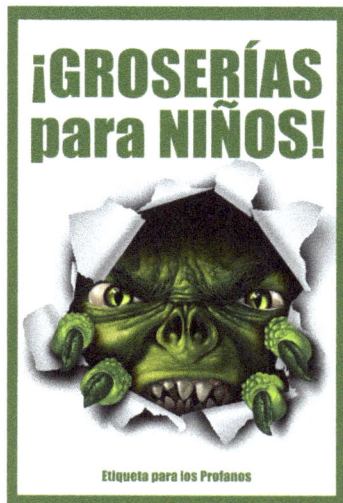

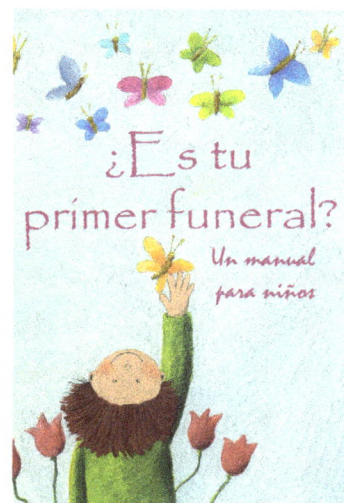

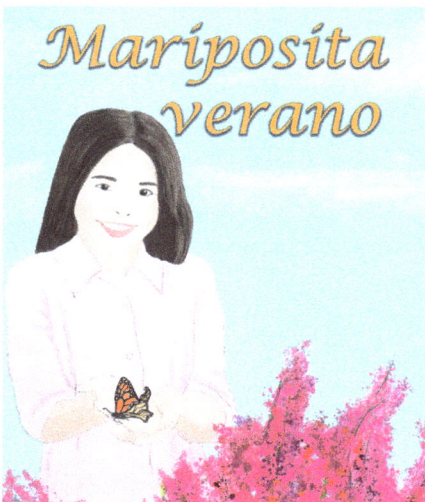

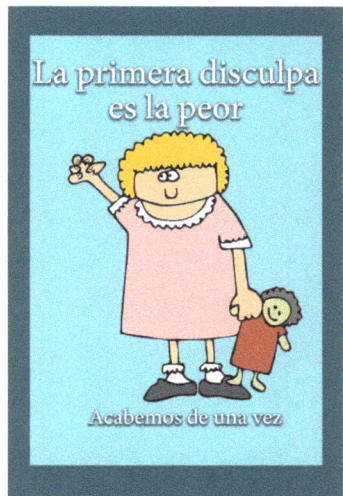

www.ingramcontent.com/pod-product-compliance
Lightning Source LLC
Chambersburg PA
CBHW042335030426
42335CB00027B/3352